SUPERSTRUCTURES

Bridges

Chris Oxlade

RSVP

RAINTREE
STECK-VAUGHN
P U B L I S H E R S
The Steck-Vaughn Company

Austin, Texas

Published by Raintree Steck-Vaughn Publishers, an imprint of Steck-Vaughn Company

Library of Congress Cataloging-in-Publication Data
    Oxlade, Chris.
    Bridges / Chris Oxlade.
      p.   cm. — (Superstructures)
    Includes index.
    Summary: Describes different types of bridges around the world and throughout history and how they are built.
    ISBN 0-8172-4331-3
    1. Bridges — Juvenile literature.   [1. Bridges.]   I. Title.   II. Series.
TG148.O94   1997
624'.2 — dc20   96-10849
                                                CIP   AC

Printed in Spain
Bound in the United States
1 2 3 4 5 6 7 8 9 0 LB 99 98 97 96

Designers: Steve Wilson, Maria D'Orsi
Series Designer: Hayley Cove
Editor: Christine Hatt
Illustrator: Martin Woodward
Picture researcher: Diana Morris
Consultant: Conor Murphy

Photographic credits
J. Allan Cash Ltd: 11, 13, 19, 25.
Collections/Brian Shuel: 10
Military Picture Library: 35
© Superstock: cover
Zefa: 14

The publishers would also like to thank Sheilagh Chadfield of Cleveland Structural Engineering Limited for her help throughout the project.

Note to the reader:
Words in **bold** appear in the glossary on page 46.

Contents

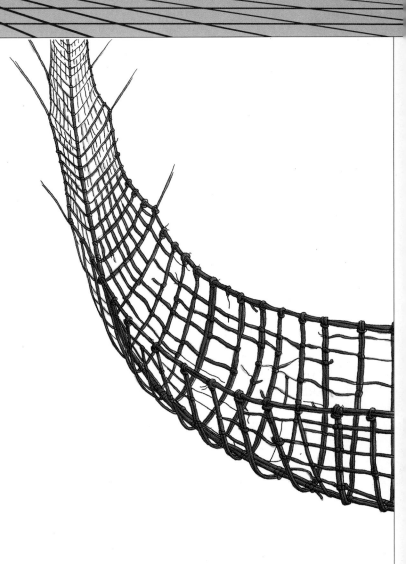

Bridges

At some time during most car and train trips, we cross over or go under a bridge. Bridges carry vehicles and people quickly and easily over obstacles such as rivers, valleys, roads, and railroads. They are an important part of a country's transportation system. Bridges over rivers make a slow ferry ride or a long **detour** unnecessary. Bridges over valleys mean that roads and railroads do not have to be built up and down steep slopes. Bridges over roads and railroads mean that cars and trains do not have to stop to let other vehicles pass.

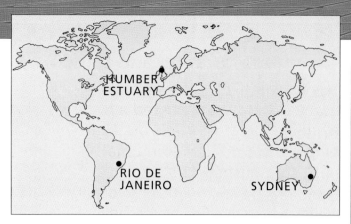

Rio-Niteroi Bridge Factfile

Structure: Box girder beam
Overall length: 9 miles (14km)
Central span: 985 feet (300m)
Height in middle: 207 feet (63m)
Completed: 1974
Architect: Redpath Dorman Long/Cleveland Bridge and Engineering Co.

The vast Rio-Niteroi Bridge connects Rio de Janeiro and Niteroi in Brazil. It is the longest beam bridge in the world.

The Humber Bridge is a suspension bridge over the Humber Estuary in the north of England. In 1995, it was still the longest bridge in the world.

What kind of bridge?

You have probably seen many different sizes and shapes of bridges, but there are really only three types: beam bridges, arch bridges, and suspension bridges. Before they can decide which type of bridge to build, architects and engineers must find out the **span** (the distance the bridge must cover without a support), the shape of the surrounding land, and whether the bridge has to cross water. They must also think about the traffic that will use the bridge, and how much space is needed for ships, trains, or trucks to pass underneath.

Past, present, and future

The Romans were the first serious bridge builders. They constructed a huge network of roads and bridges throughout their empire. The only building materials they had were wood and stone, and with these they could only construct a long bridge by building a row of short arches side by side. Arch bridges remained the main type of bridge until the eighteenth century, when iron was first used in bridge building. With iron, builders could construct beam and suspension bridges. Almost all modern bridges are built of steel and concrete. These materials, and better construction techniques, allow longer bridges than ever before to be built. Small bridges can be constructed more quickly, too.

▼ **Sydney Harbour Bridge Factfile**

Structure:	Steel arch
Length of arch:	1,650 feet (503m)
Height in middle:	170 feet (52m)
Width of roadway:	160 feet (49m)
Completed:	1932
Architect:	Redpath Dorman Long

Humber Bridge Factfile ▼

Structure:	Steel deck suspended under steel cables
Overall length:	7,280 feet (2220m)
Central span:	4,625 feet (1410m)
Height in middle:	98 feet (30m)
Height of towers:	533 feet (162.5m)
Completed:	1981
Architect:	Freeman Fox and Partners

The Sydney Harbour Bridge in Sydney, Australia, carries both road and railroad traffic and is the widest bridge in the world.

STEP BY STEP

In this space on each double page we show you a stage in the building of an imaginary beam bridge. The sequence starts here and ends on page 21.

1 Before bridge building can start, geologists must survey the site. They test the ground by drilling **boreholes** with a rig.

Beam Bridges

A beam bridge is made of one or more beams — long pieces of wood, concrete, or other building material — supported at each end. Beam bridges can be as simple as a log laid over a stream, or as complex as a long road bridge with several beams and supports made from concrete and steel. Here and on the following eight pages, you can find out how beam bridges work and the different methods and materials that are used to build them.

A single span beam bridge is supported at either end, but has no piers in the middle.

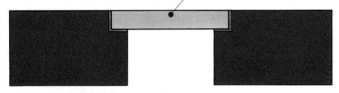

SHORT SINGLE SPAN

A multiple span beam bridge is supported at the ends and by piers between spans.

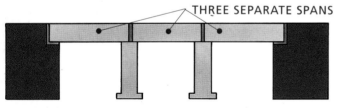

THREE SEPARATE SPANS

A continuous span beam bridge is supported both at the ends and by piers in the middle.

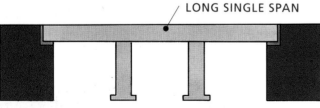

LONG SINGLE SPAN

The weight of traffic causes compression and tension in beams.

WEIGHT

COMPRESSION

TENSION

How a beam bridge works

The forces on a bridge are called loads. Live load is the weight of the traffic, dead load is the weight of the bridge, and wind load is the force of the wind. When there is live load on a beam, the beam bends down. As it bends, the material in the top of the beam is squashed (this is called **compression**), and the material in the bottom is stretched (this is called **tension**). If it bends too much, the beam collapses.

Parts of a beam bridge

Many beam bridges have one central span and two side spans. Each span is made up of several concrete beams, and the **deck** is laid on the top. The beams are supported by **piers** and **abutments**, which rest on solid underground **foundations**.

Beam bridges are the most common bridge type and often carry a minor road over a highway. This one has a central span and two side spans.

ABUTMENT

CONCRETE BEAMS SUPPORT DECK

CENTRAL SPAN

DECK MADE FROM SLAB OF CONCRETE

SIDE SPAN

PIER

Expanding and contracting

Most materials expand (grow longer) as the temperature rises, and contract (grow shorter) as it falls. Bridge beams behave like this as the weather changes from hot to cold. They also bend slightly as traffic crosses over them. If the ends of beams were fixed in place, this expanding, contracting, and bending would make them crack. So beams rest on special sliding pads called bearing plates that allow them to move slightly. The deck also has expansion joints that allow parts of it to expand and then contract without cracking.

Expansion joints are made of layers of rubber folded in an accordian shape between steel plates.

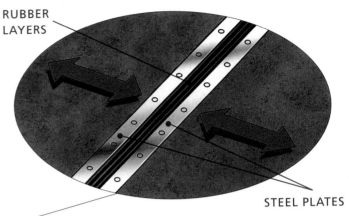

RUBBER LAYERS

STEEL PLATES

EXPANSION JOINT

BEARING PLATE

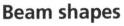

RUBBER PADS

STEEL PLATES

BOLT HOLES

Bearing plates consist of rubber pads between steel plates that are bolted firmly into position.

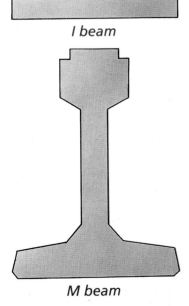

I beam

M beam

Beam shapes

The shape of a beam is designed to prevent it from bending too much, and to keep it as lightweight as possible. The more vehicles a beam has to support and the longer it is, the deeper and heavier it also needs to be. It is impossible to build extremely long beam bridges because the beams would have to be so thick that they would collapse under their own weight.

One common type of steel beam is called an I beam. Its cross section (seen by looking at the beam from the end) makes it very strong for its weight. Concrete M beams are also widely used.

STEP BY STEP

2 Watertight **cofferdams** are built in the riverbed. These keep the water out while engineers build the bridge's pile foundations.

Firm Foundations

Hidden in the ground under every bridge is one of its most important parts – the foundations. The foundations support the weight of the bridge and the traffic on it, carrying it down into solid ground. If there were no foundations, the bridge supports would probably sink, making the bridge collapse. Piers and abutments support the beams in a beam bridge. In turn, the underground foundations support the piers and abutments.

Choosing foundations

There are several different types of foundation. The type chosen for a bridge depends on the weight each bridge pier will have to carry and the **geology** – the type of soil and rock – of the ground. A geological survey is always carried out before the bridge is built. It may reveal an area of solid rock, layers of different types of rock, or deep, soft soil.

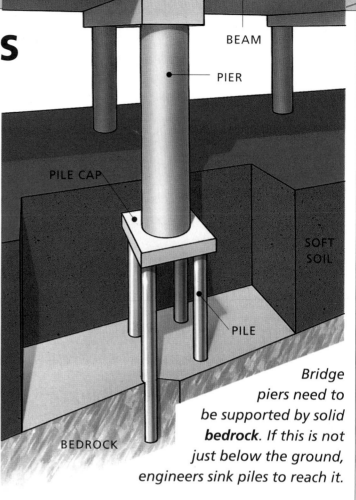

*Bridge piers need to be supported by solid **bedrock**. If this is not just below the ground, engineers sink piles to reach it.*

Rock solid

The firmest foundations rest on solid rock. If there is solid rock near the surface, the base for a pier can be built directly on top of it. If the solid rock is deeper down, buried under layers of soil, long steel or concrete columns, called **piles**, are sunk instead. They reach right down to the solid rock, and the piers rest on top of them.

Concrete rafts

Where the soil underneath a bridge pier is deep and soft, special foundations are needed to spread out the bridge's weight, so that the ground does not sag under it. One way of doing this is to build a massive concrete slab, called a **raft**. This is also called a floating. It allows the bridge to "float" on top of the soil.

Concrete rafts or floatings are used to support piers when solid rock is far below the ground and cannot be easily reached by piles.

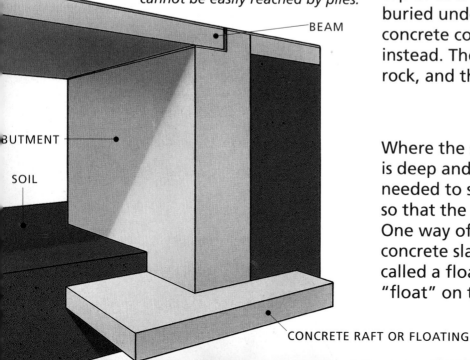

Building in shallow water

Beam bridges can be constructed across areas of shallow water by building a series of piers in the water. First, the water must be temporarily moved aside to excavate and build the foundations. In very shallow water, a cofferdam is built around the site of the foundation, and the water is pumped out.

A cofferdam is made by driving interlocking steel plates into the riverbed.

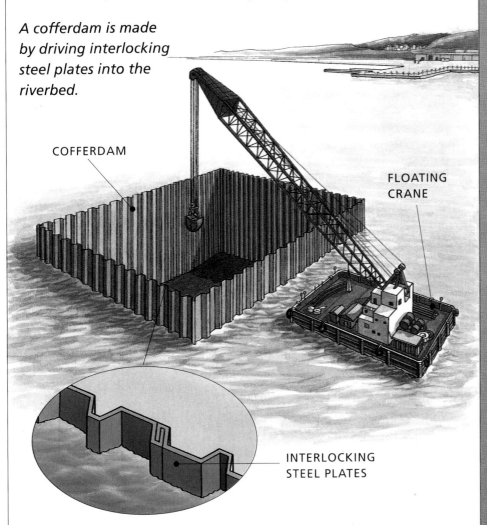

COFFERDAM

FLOATING CRANE

INTERLOCKING STEEL PLATES

Building in deep water

In deeper water, a structure called a caisson is used. A caisson is a huge concrete or steel tube that reaches from the surface down to the riverbed. **Silt** from the riverbed is dug out by cranes, or by workers inside a pressurized compartment in the bottom of the caisson. When the caisson is finally resting on solid rock, it is weighted down with **ballast**, such as concrete, to keep it in place. It then forms a solid base for the piers.

Open-ended caissons are built directly on to solid bedrock underneath deep water.

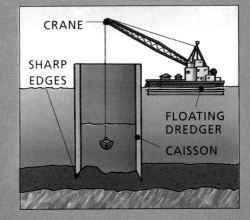

CRANE

SHARP EDGES

FLOATING DREDGER

CAISSON

*1 The sharp edges of the caisson help it to sink as a crane on a **dredger** digs silt from the river.*

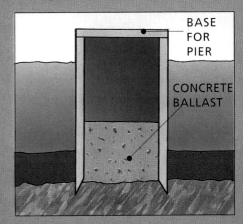

BASE FOR PIER

CONCRETE BALLAST

2 Once in place, the caisson is weighted down with ballast and a pier base is built on top.

STEP BY STEP

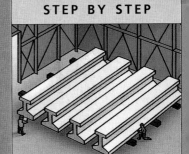

3 Massive prestressed concrete beams for the bridge are manufactured in a factory and later transported to the site.

Concrete Beams

Concrete is the material most commonly used for bridge building. It is made by mixing stones, or **aggregate**, cement, and water. The mixture gradually sets, producing a very hard, long-lasting material. To make beams, fresh concrete is poured into molds, then left to set. Concrete is also used to build other parts of a bridge, such as the foundations, the piers, and the deck. It is usually strengthened with steel bars rather than used on its own.

This typical concrete beam bridge spans a section of the M25, the highway that surrounds London.

Reinforced concrete

Concrete is extremely difficult to squash (it is strong in compression), but easier to pull apart (it is weak in tension). By itself, it would be useless for making beams that are both squashed and pulled by loads. To make beams stronger, steel bars are added where the concrete would be in tension. This combination of concrete and steel is called reinforced concrete. The steel in most bridge beams is stretched, either before the concrete sets (prestressing), or after it sets (post-stressing). This makes a beam even stronger.

PRESTRESSING CONCRETE

*1 First, a steel bar is pulled from both ends until taut. This process is called **tensioning**.*

2 Next the tensioned bar is placed inside a wood mold, and concrete poured over it.

3 Once the concrete is set, the steel is released and the wooden mold removed.

POST-STRESSING CONCRETE

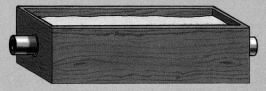

1 Concrete is poured into a mold containing a hollow tube, then left to set.

2 The mold is removed, then a steel bar is threaded through the tube and tensioned.

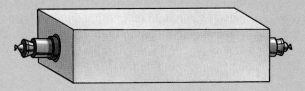

3 A grip is attached to the steel bar to keep it tensioned. This process is called tying off.

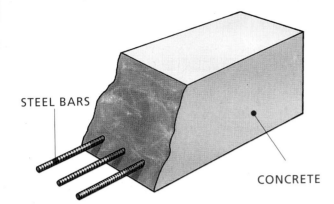

This cross section of a concrete beam shows the position of the reinforcing steel bars.

Precast concrete

Precast concrete is molded in a factory away from the building site. Many bridges are built with standard-sized, precast beams. For other bridges, precast beams have to be specially made. The standard-sized beams are much cheaper. Precast beams are normally prestressed, too.

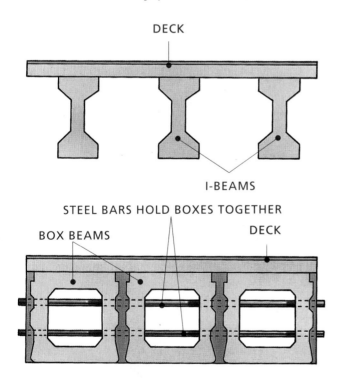

Precast concrete I beams or box beams are often used to build decks. The beams are placed side by side and the deck is built in situ on the top.

A complex wood framework like this is called **formwork**. It acts as a mold for in situ concrete.

In situ concrete

Concrete made at a building site is called **in situ concrete**. This is used to construct the deck, piers, and abutments and to strengthen the precast beams. Very large or complicated beams are normally also made in situ, since they would be difficult to transport from a factory.

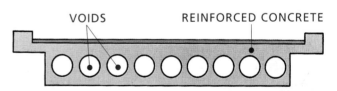

A deck can also be built using a voided slab. This is a type of concrete beam and deck combined that contains tube-shaped voids (holes). These make the slabs lighter without losing much of their strength.

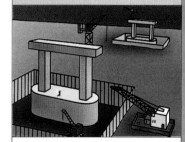

STEP BY STEP

4 Concrete piers for the new bridge are built on top of the pile foundations that have been driven deep into the riverbed.

Girders and Trusses

Most short bridges are made with simple concrete beams, but there are other ways of making beams and using them to build bridges. On these two pages you can see several of the most common. Some may look complicated, but they still work in the same way as simple concrete beams.

Steel girders

Steel plate girders are similar to concrete beams, but they are made by **welding** or bolting together flat sheets of steel. Plate girders are sometimes used instead of concrete beams, but in the same way. They are placed side by side and a concrete deck is molded on top. Plate girders are often used to build short railroad bridges.

Building a plate girder railroad bridge. The two large girders will form the basic structure of the bridge. Smaller girders resting between them will support the track.

Trusses

A **truss** is a beam made by joining lengths of steel called **struts** and **ties** to form a framework. Trusses are more complicated to build than plate girders, but they are much lighter and use less steel. Truss bridges normally consist of two trusses, with the deck supported between them. Today, trusses are more often used for small, temporary bridges than for large, permanent ones. This is because they are easy to transport in small pieces and relatively simple to construct on site.

Close-up of a plate girder

PLATE GIRDERS

REINFORCED CONCRETE PIERS

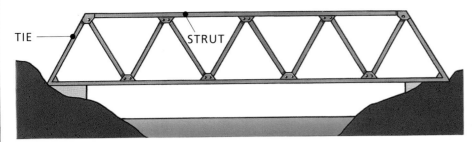

TIE — STRUT

In a truss (left), the struts and ties are held together at the ends with bolts. The triangular shapes formed by the struts and ties keep the whole truss in shape.

This truss railroad bridge carries trains over the Ogun River near Ibadan in western Nigeria.

A cross section of a box girder (right). The shape is like two beams placed side by side.

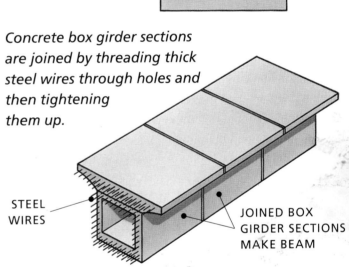

BOX GIRDER

Concrete box girder sections are joined by threading thick steel wires through holes and then tightening them up.

STEEL WIRES

JOINED BOX GIRDER SECTIONS MAKE BEAM

Box girders

A **box girder** is a beam with a cross section in the shape of a box. This shape makes it very stiff and strong. Box girders are normally used for long beam bridges and are large enough to carry a road or railroad on top. They can be made from thin steel plates that are welded together, or from molded concrete. Box girders are normally made in short sections in a factory and then joined together later to make a box girder bridge. A concrete deck is laid over the joined girder sections.

This concrete box girder bridge carries a road over a valley.

STEP BY STEP

5 Massive concrete abutments are built on both the riverbanks to provide strong support for the bridge beams.

Cantilever Bridges

A cantilever is a beam supported at only one end. The other end hangs freely in midair. A simple cantilever bridge has two cantilever arms reaching into the center from piers at the sides. The cantilever arms do not fall over because the abutments at the ends of the bridge hold them down. Like other types of beams, cantilevers can be made from concrete, steel, or both.

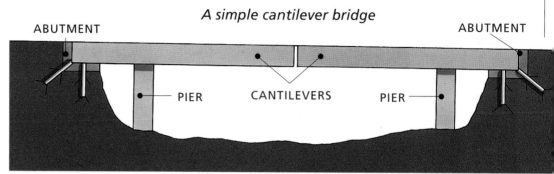

A simple cantilever bridge

ABUTMENT PIER CANTILEVERS PIER ABUTMENT

Suspended spans

Sometimes cantilevers on their own cannot make a long enough bridge. One way of making a cantilever bridge longer is to add a short beam between the ends of the two cantilever arms. A beam of this type is called a suspended span because it hangs between the cantilever arms without touching the bridge's sides.

Balanced cantilevers

Cantilevers do not have to be held down at both ends of a bridge. One cantilever arm can be balanced by another on the opposite side of a pier. This arrangement is called a balanced cantilever. A long bridge can be built by placing several balanced cantilevers end to end. It can be made even longer by adding suspended spans between each of the balanced cantilevers.

The Forth Railway Bridge in Scotland has a central balanced cantilever and two suspended spans. The cantilever arms are truss girders made by joining sections of thick steel tubing.

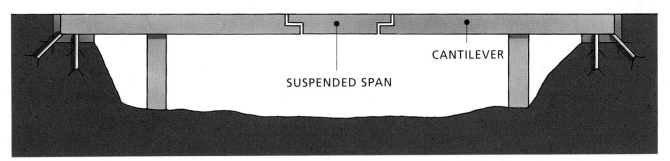

A suspended span cantilever bridge

SUSPENDED SPAN

CANTILEVER

Building cantilevers

Many modern cantilever bridges have arms made from precast concrete or steel sections. The foundations and piers of the bridges are built first. Then the cantilever arms are built out from the piers.

Perfect balance

The cantilevers are built in each direction at the same rate. The pier does not tip over because the arms always balance each other perfectly. Finally, the arms are joined with a small section called the **key**.

BUILDING A BALANCED CANTILEVER

A concrete balanced cantilever bridge is built in several stages.

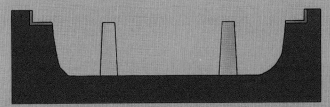

1 First, the foundations, piers, and abutments of the bridge are constructed.

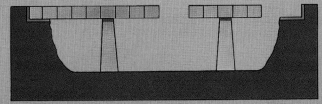

4 The cantilevers on one side are extended to the abutment and new cantilevers are then built out from the second pier.

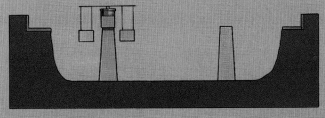

2 Next, cantilever arms are built out from both sides of one of the piers.

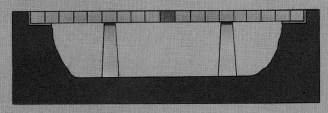

5 Finally, the key segment is added in the center, to complete the bridge.

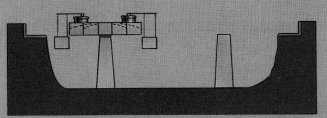

3 The sections are joined together by tightened steel wires called tendons.

STEP BY STEP

6 The concrete side beams are lifted into place by huge cranes working from the riverbanks. Slowly, the bridge is taking shape.

Arch Bridges

Arches are very simple structures that can be built from **masonry** (stone, brick, or concrete) alone, without any steel reinforcement. For this reason they are one of the oldest types of bridges. (The other is the simple stone beam.) Arch bridges may have existed more than 5,000 years ago. Few arch bridges are built today, because it is much easier and cheaper for engineers to construct cantilever or cable-stayed bridges.

Any weight on an arch bridge travels down its vertical supports, along the curve of the arch to the abutments, and down into the ground.

How an arch bridge works

You can think of an arch as a beam bent down at the ends. Weight on top of the arch is carried down to the ends and into the ground. The shape of the arch means that a load causes compression but not tension in it. This makes it possible to build an arch from masonry, which is strong in compression, but weak in tension. Any weight pushes down and out at the ends of the arch. Heavy abutments are needed to stop the arch from spreading outwards.

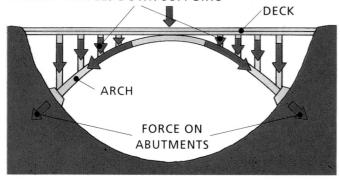

The Hell Gate Bridge, which carries rail traffic over the East River in New York, was completed in 1916.

Swiss engineer Robert Maillart designed the 1930 Salginatobel Bridge, a concrete arch in the Alps.

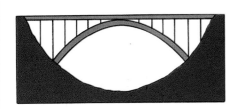

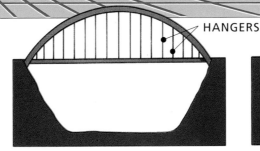

HANGERS

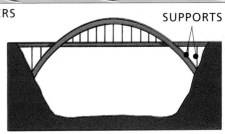

SUPPORTS

Three different types of spandrel arch. The deck can run over (left), under (center), or through (right) the arch.

Modern arches

Most modern arch bridges are made from concrete or a steel frame. Concrete arches normally have the deck resting on the top, supported by vertical columns. Steel frame arches are made by joining lengths of steel, in the same way as truss girders. Until suspension bridges were developed, the bridges with the longest spans were steel arches. Arch bridges can have a longer span than beam or cantilever bridges but are more difficult to build.

Arch bridge designs

There are several different designs of arch bridge. Old arch bridges are called solid arches because the gap between the arch and the deck is filled. A spandrel arch has a separate arch and deck, connected by **hangers** and vertical supports. The deck can hang underneath the arch, go through the arch, or sit over the arch.

Building a concrete arch

Concrete arches are normally made with in situ concrete and built from the outside into the middle. The piers at the ends of the arch are built first, then used to support the molds, called formwork, in which the concrete is left to set. Sometimes the central part of the arch is made on the ground and added in one huge piece, to complete the curved shape.

BUILDING A CONCRETE ARCH BRIDGE

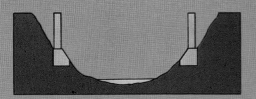

1 The abutments in the valley sides and the two piers at either end of the bridge are built first.

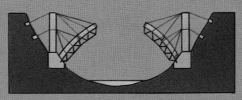

2 Next, the formwork is hung on the piers, and the arch is made using in situ concrete.

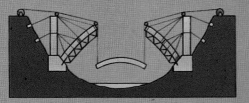

*3 The center section of the concrete arch is made on the ground and lifted into place with **winches**.*

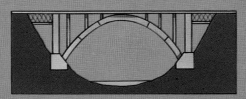

4 The concrete deck, side beams, and more piers are added to complete the new bridge.

STEP BY STEP

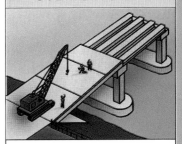

7 Once the side beams are securely in place, the deck can be added over them. It is constructed using in situ concrete.

Suspension Bridges

The bridges with the longest spans in the world are all suspension bridges. In a suspension bridge, the deck hangs from long cables. Spans of over 1 mile (1km) are quite common. A bridge with a central span of over 1 mile (1.6km) is due to open in Japan in 1998. There is no reason why longer spans should not be built. A bridge over 2 miles (3km) long between Italy and Sicily is already planned. Suspension bridges are used to cross wide, deep rivers, or even seas.

How a supension bridge works

A suspension bridge has four main parts. These are the towers (sometimes called pylons), cables, hangers (sometimes called suspenders), and deck. The weight of the vehicles traveling over the deck of a suspension bridge pulls down on the cables, trying to stretch them. In turn, the cables pull down and sideways on the towers. But the towers do not fall inward because the cables are attached to extremely strong **anchors** on the bank.

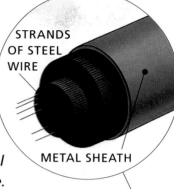

Suspension bridge cables are made of thousands of strands of steel wire bundled together. The strands are protected by a metal sheath around the cable. A single cable may be over 1 yard (1m) thick.

STRANDS OF STEEL WIRE

METAL SHEATH

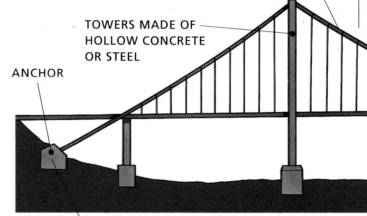

TOWERS MADE OF HOLLOW CONCRETE OR STEEL

ANCHOR

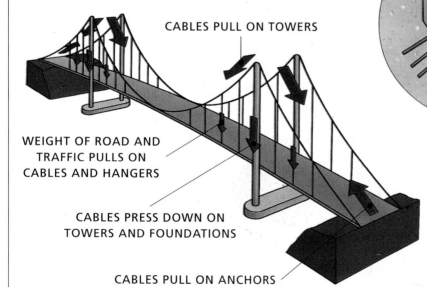

CABLES PULL ON TOWERS

WEIGHT OF ROAD AND TRAFFIC PULLS ON CABLES AND HANGERS

CABLES PRESS DOWN ON TOWERS AND FOUNDATIONS

CABLES PULL ON ANCHORS

CABLE

ANCHOR BOLT

The ends of the bridge cables are secured in the anchors. Where possible, the anchors are set in solid rock on the riverbank. Where there is no rock, massive slabs of concrete, often as big as apartment buildings, are built instead.

The weight of a suspension bridge and its traffic load pulls down on the bridge cables. The cables pull on the towers. But these do not fall down because anchors hold the cables in position.

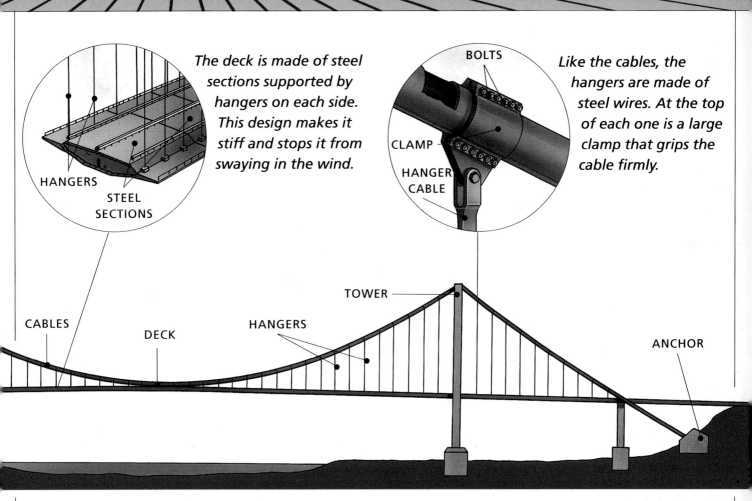

The deck is made of steel sections supported by hangers on each side. This design makes it stiff and stops it from swaying in the wind.

HANGERS

STEEL SECTIONS

BOLTS

CLAMP

HANGER CABLE

Like the cables, the hangers are made of steel wires. At the top of each one is a large clamp that grips the cable firmly.

CABLES

DECK

HANGERS

TOWER

ANCHOR

Simple suspensions

Not all suspension bridges are complicated concrete and steel structures. In many parts of the world, simple suspension bridges carry paths over rivers. The cables, which can be made of either thick rope or steel, form part of the walkway.

This simple rope suspension bridge crosses the River Mahaweli in Kandy, Sri Lanka.

This diagram of a suspension bridge highlights its essential parts — cables, towers, hangers, and deck. The anchors in the river-bank are also essential. Without them, the bridge would collapse.

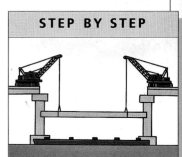

STEP BY STEP

8 Once the deck covers the side beams, the central span beams are lifted up from a barge in the river by cranes.

Building a Suspension Bridge

The construction of a large suspension bridge is a major civil engineering project. Suspension bridges are normally built over water, and the building site can be several miles long. This makes construction more difficult than on land. Foundations and piers usually have to be built in water, and workers and building materials have to be carefully organized.

Deciding where to build

Choosing the right place to build this kind of a suspension bridge is very important. It is not always possible to build it in the most convenient place for traffic. The river may be so wide or deep there that the bridge would be too expensive to build. Or the type of ground at that site may make it difficult to build solid foundations. It is often cheaper and easier to move farther along the river, and build new roads to reach the ends of the bridge.

Many suspension bridges have steel towers. These are made in sections that are hoisted into place by cranes at the building site and joined together.

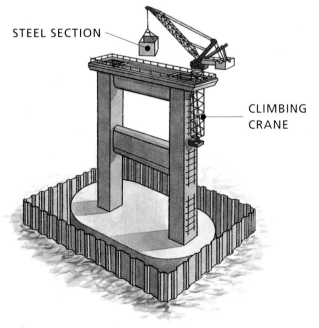

STEEL SECTION

CLIMBING CRANE

BUILDING STAGES

1 First, the foundations, piers, and anchors of the suspension bridge are built. These will give the bridge a strong, solid base.

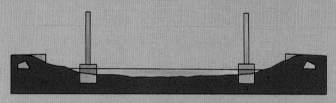

2 Next, the twin towers are built on top of the piers. These may be made of steel or concrete and will support the massive cables.

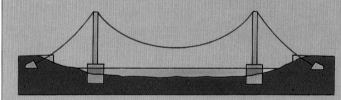

3 The two thick steel cables are added, going over the towers and down to the anchors, which are embedded in the riverbank.

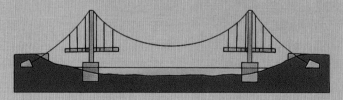

4 The deck is added in sections. Work may begin at the towers and move out, or at the ends and middle and move toward the towers.

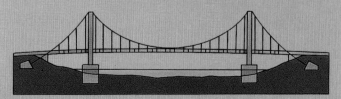

5 Once the deck is complete, the road surface is added, preparing the new suspension bridge for cars, trucks, and other traffic.

The building process

Different parts of a suspension bridge are always built in the same order. The foundations, piers, and anchors are built first, followed by the towers. When these are completed, the cables are hung over the towers and attached to the anchors. Once the cables are in place, the deck is added piece by piece. While the bridge itself is being built, the **approach roads** are constructed on the riverbanks.

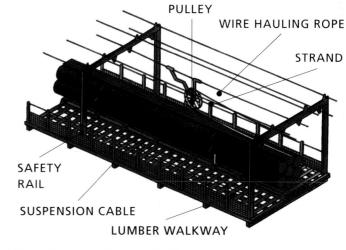

PULLEY
WIRE HAULING ROPE
STRAND
SAFETY RAIL
SUSPENSION CABLE
LUMBER WALKWAY

The bridge cables are built up strand by strand. This is called spinning. Each strand is put over a pulley, which crosses the bridge on a wire. When the pulley reaches the other side, the strand is taken off, and the pulley returns for a new strand.

Each deck section is hauled into place by tugboats on the water, then attached to its hangers. The deck sections are not normally joined until they are all in position.

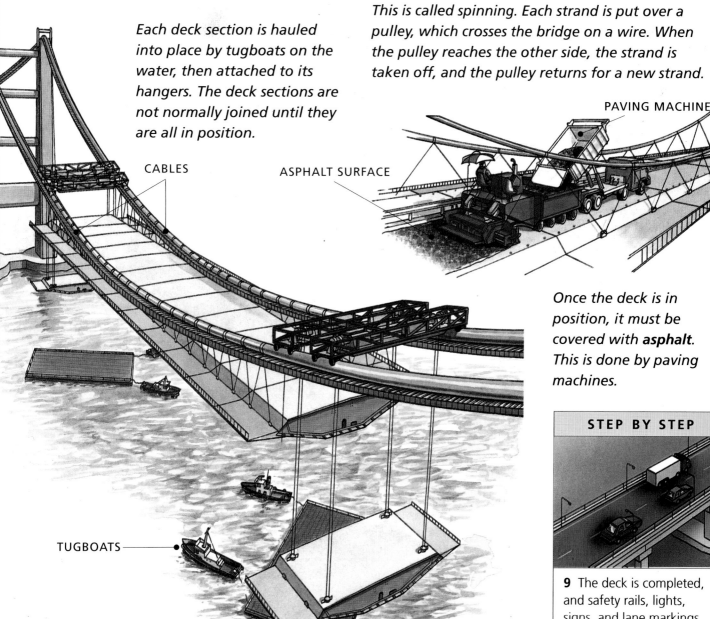

CABLES

ASPHALT SURFACE

PAVING MACHINE

TUGBOATS

*Once the deck is in position, it must be covered with **asphalt**. This is done by paving machines.*

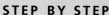

STEP BY STEP

9 The deck is completed, and safety rails, lights, signs, and lane markings are all added. Finally, the bridge is opened to traffic.

Cable-Stayed Bridges

Cable-stayed bridges are built in a similar way to suspension bridges. But the deck sections are not hung under a cable strung over the towers, as in a suspension bridge. Instead, each section is supported by its own cable attached to a tower. Cable-stayed bridges are popular for medium-length bridges with a total span of between about 660 feet (200m) and 2,600 feet (800m).

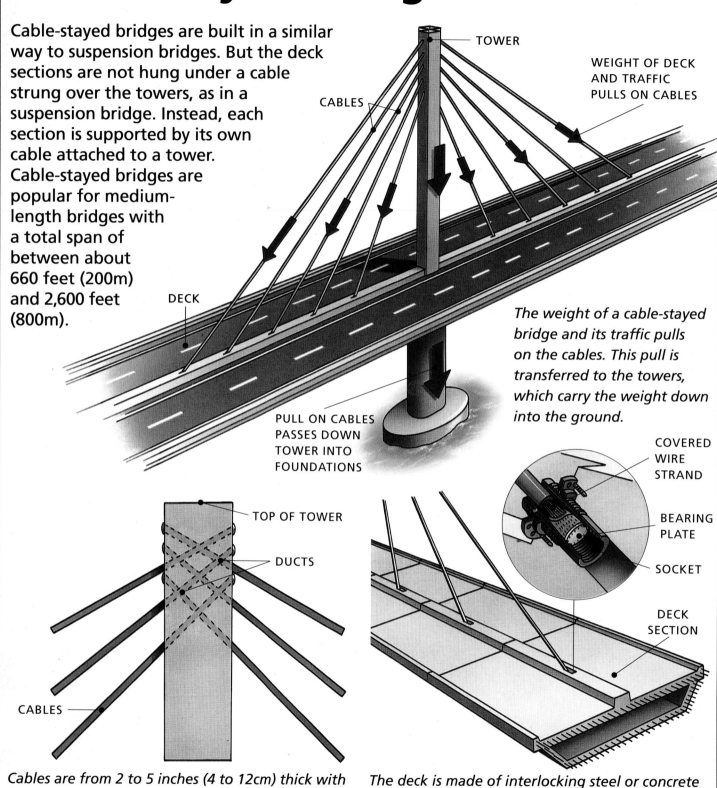

TOWER

WEIGHT OF DECK AND TRAFFIC PULLS ON CABLES

CABLES

DECK

PULL ON CABLES PASSES DOWN TOWER INTO FOUNDATIONS

The weight of a cable-stayed bridge and its traffic pulls on the cables. This pull is transferred to the towers, which carry the weight down into the ground.

TOP OF TOWER

DUCTS

CABLES

COVERED WIRE STRAND

BEARING PLATE

SOCKET

DECK SECTION

*Cables are from 2 to 5 inches (4 to 12cm) thick with many wire strands. They are fed into **ducts** at the top of concrete towers to hold them in place.*

The deck is made of interlocking steel or concrete sections similar to those in suspension bridges. The sections are linked to the cables with strong joints.

Parts of a cable-stayed bridge

A cable-stayed bridge has three main parts. These are the towers (sometimes called pylons), the deck, and the cables. The towers and the cables in a suspension bridge can be arranged in only one way. But there are many possible arrangements of towers and cables in a cable-stayed bridge. Often the cables are attached to the center of the deck, but they may also be attached on both sides.

How a cable-stayed bridge works

Each deck section of a cable-stayed bridge pulls downwards like a **pendulum** on its cable. This makes the cables pull down and sideways on the towers, which carry the weight into the ground. The sideways pull on one side of the tower is balanced by the sideways pull on the other. Each deck section leans on whichever neighboring section is closer to a tower. This holds the deck together and means it is not necessary to have strong connections between the sections.

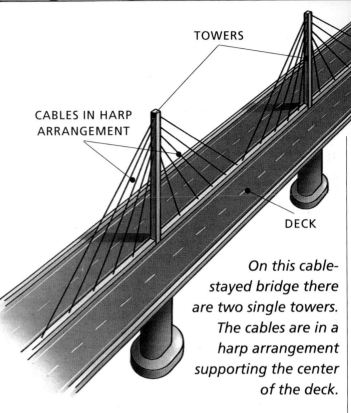

TOWERS

CABLES IN HARP ARRANGEMENT

DECK

On this cable-stayed bridge there are two single towers. The cables are in a harp arrangement supporting the center of the deck.

Building a cable-stayed bridge

The building of a cable-stayed bridge begins with the foundations, piers, and towers. Then the deck sections are added with their cables, one on each side of a tower at a time, to provide balance.

This cable-stayed bridge has an A-frame tower with twin sets of cables attached to both sides of the deck.

A-FRAME TOWER

DECK

TWIN SETS OF CABLES

STEP BY STEP

In this space on each double page, we show you a stage in the building of an imaginary cable-stayed bridge. The sequence starts here and ends on page 39.

1 The foundations are built inside caissons that have been sunk to the riverbed. Supporting piers are built on top of the foundations.

The First Bridges

The first people on Earth were hunter-gatherers, who moved from place to place searching for food. They probably used natural bridges, such as branches or fallen tree trunks, to help them cross rivers. In about 10,000 BC, people began to farm. Groups of people settled in different places and began to trade with one another. Routes between settlements were used regularly. This is when simple, permanent bridges were probably first built. To construct them, early people used natural materials, such as wood and stone.

Simple suspension bridges like this one use building techniques invented many thousands of years ago. The vines are anchored to trees at each end of the bridge.

Clapper bridges

Wooden beam and cantilever bridges were easy to build, but the wood rotted quickly, and the bridges often had to be repaired. People overcame this problem by making the beams from stone. Some simple stone beam bridges, called clapper bridges, still exist today. But stone has disadvantages, too. It can only be used for short spans, and it is heavy and brittle, making it snap very easily.

Simple suspensions

Simple suspension bridges were probably in use more than 10,000 years ago, making them one of the oldest bridge types. They were built in places where creepers and vines were available to make the basic suspension "cables." One early design consisted of two of these cables with logs tied on top to make a walkway.

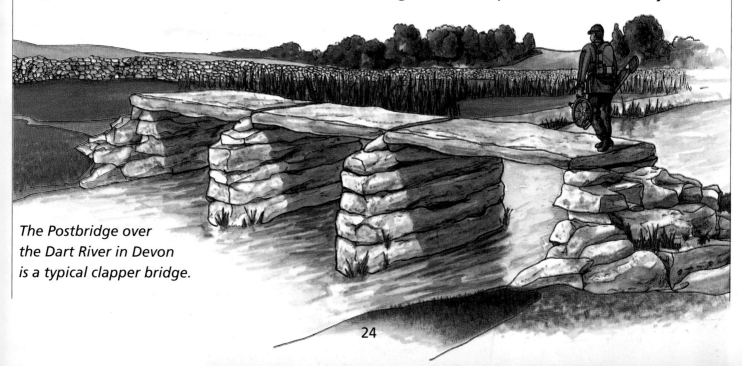

The Postbridge over the Dart River in Devon is a typical clapper bridge.

Arches and the Empire

The Roman Empire, which lasted from the first century BC to the fifth century AD, might not have been so successful without the arch bridge. The Romans had a huge road network that allowed troops and communications to travel swiftly through their vast empire. All along this network, they built thousands of arch bridges.

The Romans invented the cofferdam so that they could build bridge piers in rivers. Each dam was made using a ring of wooden stakes that were chained together and driven into the riverbed.

Roman building techniques

Most Roman bridges had several arches, with piers standing in the water below. As time went by, the Roman engineers learned how to build longer arches and narrower piers. They wanted to do this because wide piers blocked too much of a river, making it more likely that the bridge would be washed away if there were a flood. The Romans also developed cement to bind stones together.

WOODEN STAKES

CHAINS

The magnificent stone arch bridge built by the Romans in Salamanca, northern Spain, has survived to this day.

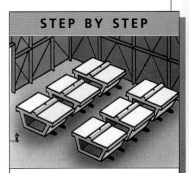

STEP BY STEP

2 Concrete sections for the bridge's deck are built ahead in a factory. Their **aerodynamic** shape stops the bridge from swaying.

Medieval and Renaissance Bridges

After the Roman Empire collapsed in about AD 400, Europe went through a period of unrest called the Middle Ages. The bridge building knowledge of the Romans was lost, and very few new bridges were constructed. Bridge building did not begin again until after about AD 1000, but even then construction standards were well below those of Roman times.

Medieval bridges, such as the Pont Valentré over the Lot River in France (below), were built with short, semicircular or pointed arches. Many collapsed because the water flowing through the arches washed away the foundations.

Renaissance arches

During the Renaissance, the revival of learning which began in Italy in the fourteenth century, many advances were made in architecture. Engineers began to understand the science of bridge building, and learned to build longer, lower arches. These were much more graceful than the heavy, semicircular and pointed arches of medieval times. The widest medieval arches were about 32 feet (10m) wide. By the eighteenth century, it was possible to build arches 100 feet (30m) wide and just 13 feet (4m) high.

ARCH SHAPES

Medieval builders used several different shapes for their bridge arches. They borrowed the idea of ribs from cathedral builders of the same time. Ribbed arches were easier to build than flat ones.

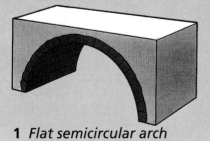

1 *Flat semicircular arch*

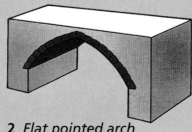

2 *Flat pointed arch*

3 *Ribbed semicircular arch*

The famous Rialto Bridge in Venice, Italy. It has a span of 85 feet (26m) and was completed in 1591.

Masonry arch bridges

Masonry arch bridges, such as the Rialto Bridge in Venice, Italy, consist of blocks of stone or concrete shaped into an arch. An arch only stays up when all the pieces are in place. So, as it is being built, the pieces must be supported. This is done by a temporary wooden arch, called a **centering**. The stones are laid around the centering until the arch is complete. The Chinese were building masonry arches of this type while Europe was still in the Middle Ages.

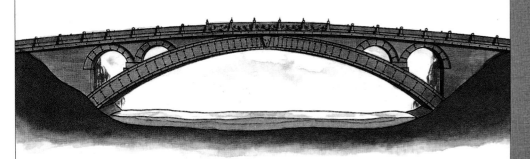

The Anji Bridge at Zhoa Xian, China, is a masonry arch. It was completed in AD 610 and is still standing today.

BUILDING A STONE ARCH

1 First, the piers are constructed as supports for the new bridge.

2 Next, wooden centering is built between the piers.

3 The arch is built stone by stone over the centering.

4 Once the arch is complete, the centering is removed.

5 Finally, the roadway is added on top of the finished bridge.

STEP BY STEP

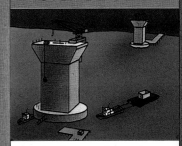

3 The first sections of the bridge's deck are built on top of the piers. These will provide a base for the bridge towers.

Iron Bridges

Iron was the most important engineering material during the **Industrial Revolution**, which started in Europe in the middle of the eighteenth century. New methods of **smelting** large amounts of iron were developed, so iron was soon used in many industries. It was also used for trains, ships, and thousands of road and rail bridges.

Cast iron

One important type of iron used in bridge construction was **cast iron**. Cast iron is brittle and weaker in tension than in compression. Several cast-iron beam bridges collapsed, sometimes because the cast iron was faulty. Sometimes the bridges were weak because the engineers did not understand how to design them.

Wrought iron

Later, **wrought iron** was developed. It is not brittle in the same way as cast iron and is much stronger than cast iron in tension. As a result, it made much more reliable beams. But cast iron was still used for bridge columns and arches.

Iron arches

The first iron bridges were arch bridges. Engineers quickly realized that iron could be used instead of masonry to build them. Iron's advantages were that it could be cast into shape, and pieces could easily be joined together with bolts. The iron arches were also lighter than masonry bridges of the same size. So they could carry more traffic without making the bridge collapse.

The world's first iron bridge, at Coalbrookdale, England. It is made of cast iron and was completed in 1779.

The Menai Strait Bridge links Wales with the island of Anglesey. It is a suspension bridge with a truss girder deck, and was completed in 1825 by the brilliant Scottish engineer Thomas Telford.

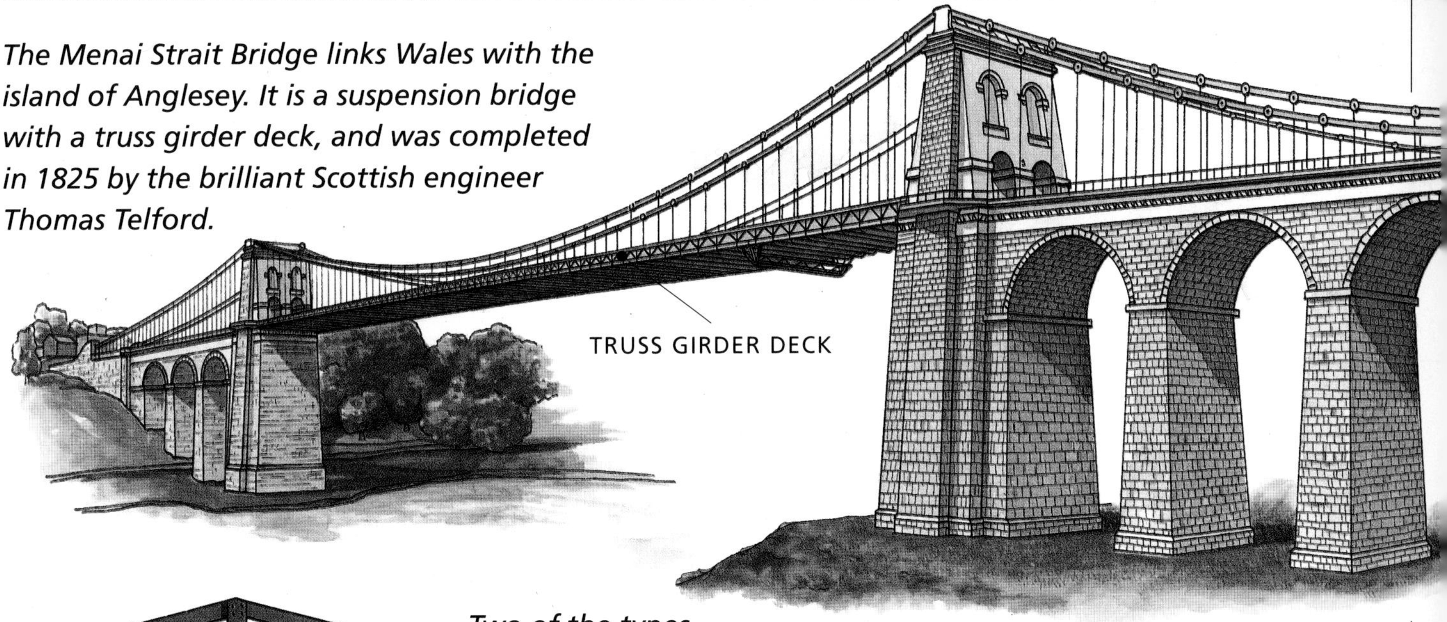

TRUSS GIRDER DECK

Two of the types of girders used in early iron beam bridges.

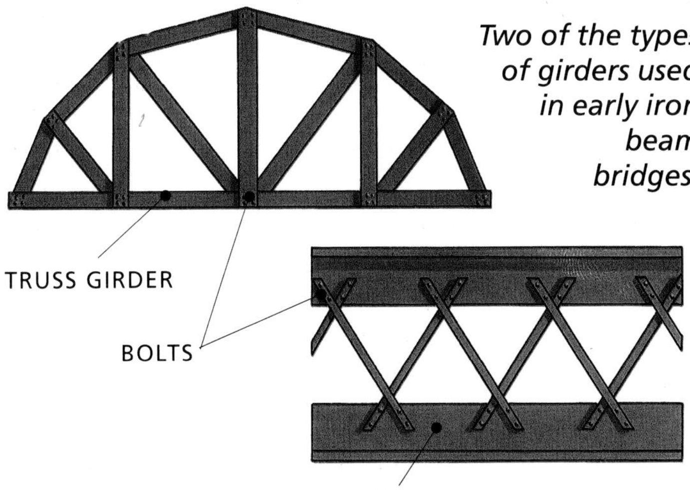

TRUSS GIRDER

BOLTS

LATTICE GIRDER

Iron for suspension

The first large suspension bridges had hangers made from iron chains. Cast iron was too brittle to make chains, so wrought iron was used instead. At that time it was impossible to make iron cables, so iron bars were joined together with iron bolts.

Iron beams

Iron is much stronger in tension than stone. This meant that iron could be used to make beams, and that long beam bridges could be built for the first time. Another new technique was to join iron plates and bars with bolts to make **truss girders** and **lattice girders** for bridge construction.

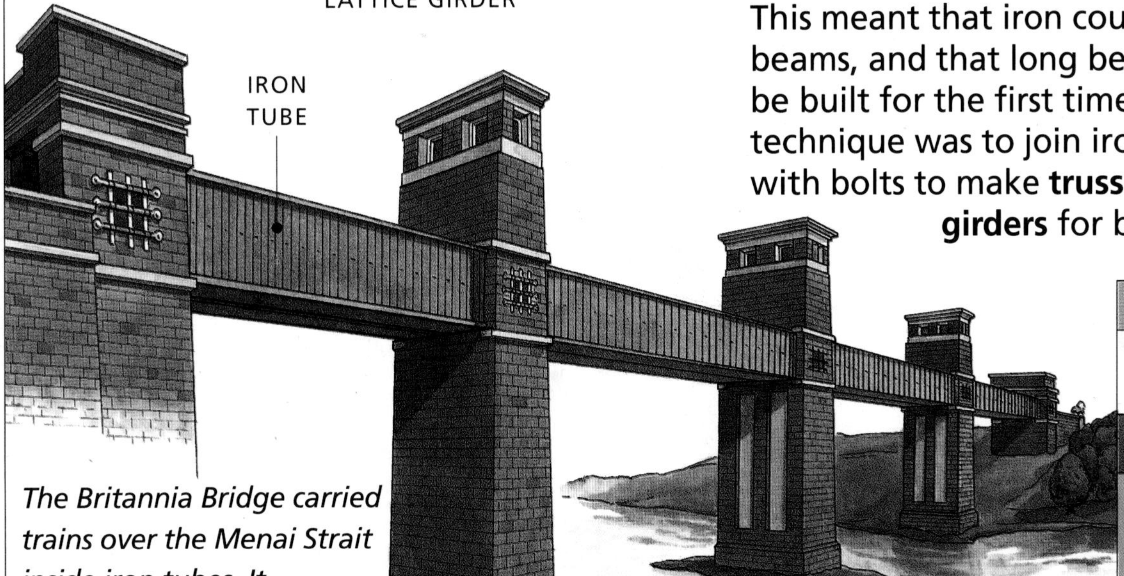

IRON TUBE

The Britannia Bridge carried trains over the Menai Strait inside iron tubes. It was designed by Robert Stephenson, and completed in 1850.

STEP BY STEP

4 The towers are built section by section on top of the piers. They will carry the bridge's weight down to the ground.

Steel and Concrete Bridges

Almost all modern bridges are made from concrete or steel, or a mixture of both materials. Steel production began in the middle of the nineteenth century, and steel soon replaced iron as a construction material. Steel was added to concrete to make reinforced concrete. Steel and concrete made bridge building easier, and allowed new forms of bridge to be built.

Steel replaces iron

Steel is an **alloy** made mainly from iron, with a small amount of carbon and other metals added to it. It is stronger than cast- or wrought iron, but not brittle, and is easy to shape when heated. A way of producing steel cheaply and in large quantities was invented in 1856 by Henry Bessemer, an English engineer. This is called the Bessemer process.

The striking, orange-painted Golden Gate Bridge in San Francisco, opened in 1937. It is a steel suspension bridge with a total length of 4,200 feet (1,280m). Its massive steel towers are 750 feet (227m) high and each cable weighs more than 7,000 tons.

The Brooklyn Bridge, in New York, (above) was opened in 1883. It was the first bridge to use steel cables. These contain nearly 1,250 miles (2,000km) of steel wire.

When the Bayonne Bridge between Newark and Staten Island, (left) was completed in 1931, it was the world's longest bridge. The main span of its giant steel arch measures 1,650 feet (504m).

30

Development of concrete

We often think of concrete as a modern material, but it is thousands of years old. Many Roman buildings and arch bridges were built of concrete. The cement in the concrete was made from limestone and a volcanic ash called *pozzuolana*. Modern cement produces similar concrete.

Reinforced concrete

Concrete is strong in compression but weak in tension. A pure concrete beam is no better than a stone beam. But in the 1860s, F. Joseph Monier, a French inventor, strengthened some concrete by adding steel rods, and so invented reinforced concrete. With reinforced concrete, engineers could build long, low arches, and simple concrete beams.

Steel trusses and arches

Steel replaced wrought iron for making all kinds of bridges. Girders were made by bolting steel plates together. Trusses were made by bolting steel struts and ties together. Steel arches were made in the same way. Steel's strength meant that these bridges could be longer than ever.

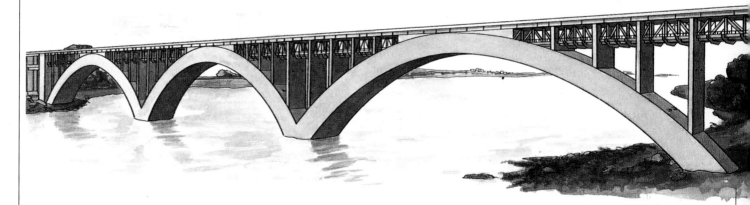

Steel for suspension

Steel cables were much stronger than iron cables, so much longer suspension bridges could be built. The first bridge with steel cables was the Brooklyn Bridge, which was completed in 1883, and has a 1,590-foot (484m) main span. It crossed the East River in New York, to join the borough of Brooklyn with Manhattan Island. Steel was also used for the hangers and the deck.

The Plougastel Bridge across the Elorn River in Brittany, northwest France. It has three reinforced concrete arches with a total span of 1,772 feet (540m), and was completed in 1930. The architect was Eugène Freyssinet.

STEP BY STEP

5 More sections of the deck are put into place on either side of the towers. Cranes lift them from barges in the river.

Toward the Future

Most modern bridges are beam, suspension, or cable-stayed bridges made of reinforced concrete or steel. Short arch bridges have been largely replaced by concrete beam bridges, and longer arches by cable-stayed bridges. It is unlikely that new types of bridge will be invented, but new materials and building methods could make future bridges lighter and longer.

New materials

A new type of reinforced concrete, called prestressed concrete, was introduced in 1945. Prestressed concrete is made by putting stretched steel bars inside concrete beams. This squeezes the concrete, making each beam much slimmer than a normal reinforced concrete beam of the same strength. The steel used in prestressed concrete is special **high-tensile steel**. Most modern concrete beam bridges are made with prestressed concrete.

The Pont de Normandie over the Seine River at Le Havre, France, was opened in 1995, and is now the longest cable-stayed bridge in the world. Its central span alone measures 2,800 feet (856m).

A modern style

Cable-stayed bridges are now popular for medium-length bridges, where spans measuring between about 660 feet (200m) and 2,600 feet (800m) are required. Longer and longer cable-stayed bridges are being built today. Civil engineers think that they could eventually reach spans of less than one mile (about 1km).

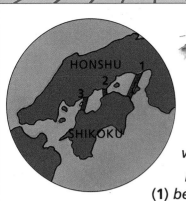

The Akashi Kaikyo Bridge will form the main part of one road link (**1**) between the islands of Shikoku and Honshu in Japan. Another road link (**2**) already exists, and a third (**3**) is planned.

Better suspension bridges

After the Brooklyn Bridge in New York was completed in 1883, more suspension bridges followed. Spans increased, and decks grew lighter and thinner. In 1940, the Tacoma Narrows suspension bridge in Washington State, collapsed after swaying violently in strong winds. As a result, engineers began to build several suspension bridges stiffened by trusses to make them stable and aerodynamic.

Choice of materials

Civil engineers think the maximum span for a heavy, steel-cabled suspension bridge will be about 1,312 feet (4,000m). However, by using synthetic fibers and lightweight materials, it may be possible to exceed even this great length in the future.

The total span of the Akashi Kaikyo Bridge will be 12,800 feet (3,910m). The bridge is designed to withstand earthquakes and strong water currents.

Longer and longer

One extremely long suspension bridge is already under construction. In 1998, the Akashi Kaikyo Bridge, Japan, will open. Its central span will be 6,530 feet (1,990m) long. But an even longer bridge is planned. Engineers hope that in the year 2004 a new bridge will be opened linking Sicily and Italy across the Messina Strait. The Messina Strait Bridge will be the longest suspension bridge in the world, with a 10,800-foot (3,300m) span. It will cost about as much as an undersea tunnel.

Building the truss-stiffened Mackinac Straits Bridge in Michigan. The bridge was completed in 1957.

STIFFENING TRUSS

STEP BY STEP

6 Each section of the deck is connected to one of the bridge cables, which is in turn is connected to a tower.

33

Special Bridges

Most modern bridges follow a regular design and are easy to build because they are like thousands of other bridges that already exist. But some bridges have to be designed specially—perhaps to let tall ships pass along a river. Some historical bridges look strange to us today because they were built for special reasons, using designs that were never needed again.

Tower Bridge in London was completed in 1894. It has two cantilevers that meet in the center, but these can be raised to let ships pass. This kind of bridge is called a bascule bridge.

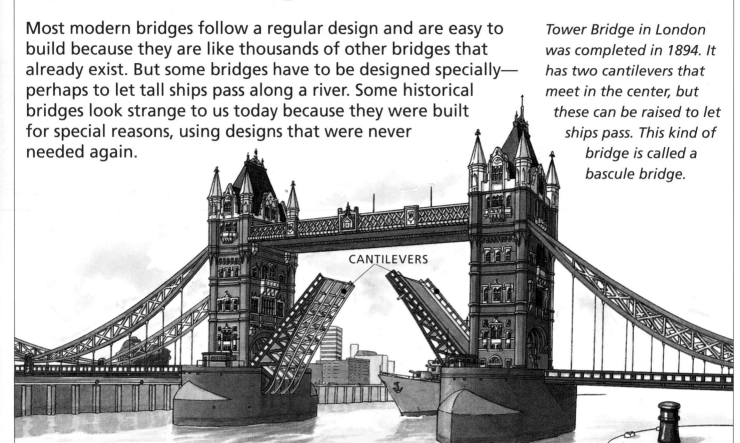

CANTILEVERS

The leaves of a swing bridge rotate to let ships through. The Low-Level Swing Bridge in Seattle, Washington, (below) was opened in 1991.

CONTROL TOWER

TWIN LEAVES MADE OF CONCRETE

Let me through!

Many bridges are built across rivers and canals. If ships will need to pass under them, engineers must allow enough headroom. Bridges for important roads are normally built on high piers so that there is always enough room, but this is too expensive for minor roads. In these cases, moving bridges are built instead. In their normal positions, these bridges cross a river or canal at low level. But when a tall ship is passing, they can be raised.

Historical oddities

In the past, engineers have experimented with many different ways of building bridges, some of them are extremely odd. The Royal Albert Bridge across the estuary of the Tamar River in Cornwall has two arches made from huge iron tubes. The construction of the bridge began in 1857 and was completed in 1859. The designer was English engineer Isambard Kingdom Brunel. His impressive bridge is still used to carry rail traffic today.

Pontoon bridges (left) are used to cross wide rivers. A pontoon bridge is supported on floats instead of piers.

There are two types of Bailey bridge. One (above) is assembled from its various parts on the spot. The other is carried complete on the back of a truck to where it is needed, then simply unfolded.

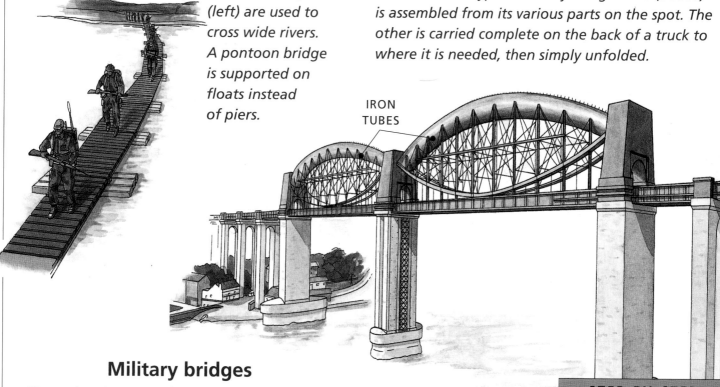

IRON TUBES

Military bridges

Military bridges are usually temporary bridges, built to allow troops and supplies to cross rivers. Because of their temporary nature, they need to be light, portable, and quick and easy to assemble and dismantle. The two most common types are the pontoon bridge, and the Bailey bridge, named after Sir Donald Bailey, who invented it in World War II.

The Royal Albert Bridge in Cornwall has a total span of 1,850 feet (563m) and towers 220 feet (67m) high. It was opened in 1859 by Prince Albert himself.

STEP BY STEP

7 More sections of the deck are added piece by piece around each tower, until the roadway is almost complete.

Viaducts and Aqueducts

A **viaduct** is a bridge that crosses a valley. It is made of a long row of arches or beams, supported on piers. Viaducts allow railroads and roads to travel over a valley, instead of having to go up and down the valley sides. The Romans were the first people to build viaducts, and the name comes from Latin words meaning "road-carrier." An aqueduct is a viaduct or bridge that carries a water pipe or a canal. Its name means "water-carrier."

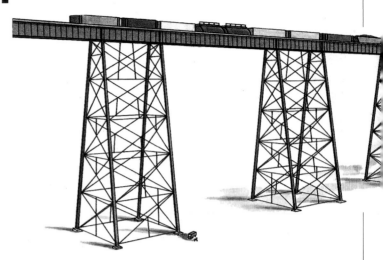

BUILDING A MULTI-LEVEL VIADUCT

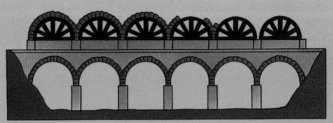

1 *The first level is built over a wooden centering supported by piers. When it is finished, the sideways forces of the arches cancel each other out, so they do not push over the piers.*

2 *The centering is removed and rebuilt at the next level in narrower arch shapes. Then stones are placed over the top in the same way as before. Finally, a third level may be added.*

Roman viaducts and aqueducts

The Romans built arch viaducts to carry roads across narrow valleys. Where a valley was very deep, they built multiple level viaducts. The spans and arches at each level were narrower than those on the level beneath them. This kept the piers short. Tall piers would have been unstable. The Romans also built many aqueducts that carried water into Rome and other cities of their massive empire.

The Pont du Gard aqueduct, near Nîmes in the south of France, was built before AD 100. Its three tiers of arches reach a height of 180 feet (55m).

The extraordinary Lethbridge Viaduct carries rail traffic across the valley of the Oldman River in Alberta, Canada. It is 1 mile (1.6km) long and 315 feet (96m) high.

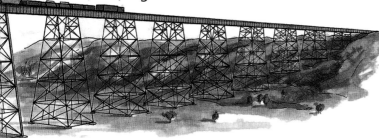

Railroad viaducts

During the nineteenth century, many thousands of miles of railroads were built in the U.S. and Europe. Hundreds of viaducts were needed to keep the new railroad networks running on a level. In Europe, most of the new viaducts were built of masonry. In the U.S., there were plentiful supplies of wood, and viaducts with wooden piers and wooden truss beams were frequently built.

This modern highway viaduct carries traffic high over railroad yards and the Tees River in the north of England. It is built from steel plate girders and has a total length of 6,350 feet (1,935m), covering 68 spans.

Bridges for water

Aqueducts are built like road or railroad bridges, but instead of a roadway or railroad on top, there is a watertight channel. Most aqueducts built to carry canals of the eighteenth and nineteenth century had channels made of iron plates.

Thomas Telford's dramatic Pont-y-Cysyllte aqueduct in Wales carries the Shropshire Union Canal over the Dee River. It was opened in 1805.

Modern viaducts

Modern viaducts are built from concrete or steel beams on top of concrete piers. Long viaducts for roads and railroads can be built reasonably cheaply because the beams can be mass-produced in a factory and then assembled on the location.

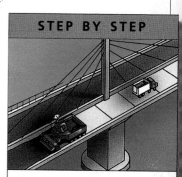

STEP BY STEP

8 The deck has to be covered with asphalt to prepare it for heavy traffic. This is done by a special paving machine.

Weird and Wonderful Bridges

During the history of bridge building, engineers have designed many weird and wonderful bridges that were never built at all. Some were far ahead of their time, while others were simply impossible to construct. Several modern examples of outrageous designs have never been built because of their great cost. But none of this stops architects and engineers from devising plans for extraordinary new bridges, because they know that if they are good enough, they may one day be constructed.

Thomas Telford designed this bridge in 1801 as a replacement for an earlier London Bridge. It was to be made of iron and have a span of nearly 656 feet (200m) — nearly three times as long as the longest iron arch of the time.

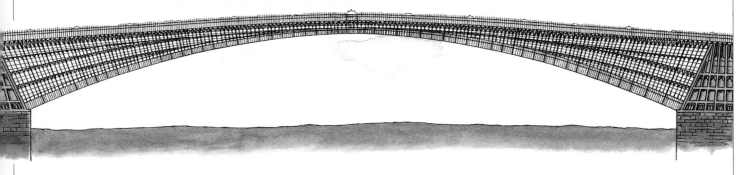

Iron London bridge

Many amazing bridges were designed in the eighteenth and nineteenth centuries. At the time, engineers were full of new ideas, but they did not really understand the science of bridge building. So often they planned spans much greater than were possible with cast or wrought iron. Thomas Telford's design for an iron bridge over the Thames River in London was sound, but he did not have enough money to build it.

*This bridge may one day span the Thames River at Greenwich during a festival to celebrate the **millennium**. The giant, helium-filled balloon bridge was designed by Michael Gold Architects.*

BALLOON WILL BE ABLE TO RISE A SHORT WAY INTO AIR

CABLES

16-FOOT- (5M-) WIDE DECK

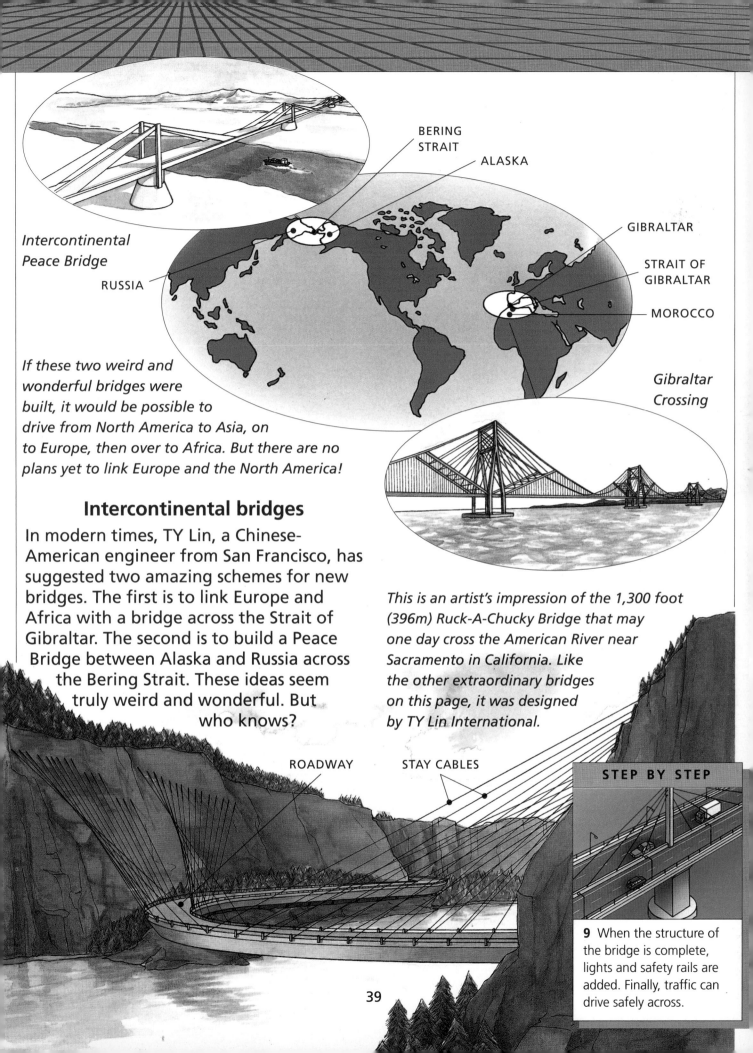

*Intercontinental
Peace Bridge*

RUSSIA

BERING
STRAIT

ALASKA

GIBRALTAR

STRAIT OF
GIBRALTAR

MOROCCO

*Gibraltar
Crossing*

*If these two weird and
wonderful bridges were
built, it would be possible to
drive from North America to Asia, on
to Europe, then over to Africa. But there are no
plans yet to link Europe and the North America!*

Intercontinental bridges

In modern times, TY Lin, a Chinese-
American engineer from San Francisco, has
suggested two amazing schemes for new
bridges. The first is to link Europe and
Africa with a bridge across the Strait of
Gibraltar. The second is to build a Peace
Bridge between Alaska and Russia across
the Bering Strait. These ideas seem
truly weird and wonderful. But
who knows?

*This is an artist's impression of the 1,300 foot
(396m) Ruck-A-Chucky Bridge that may
one day cross the American River near
Sacramento in California. Like
the other extraordinary bridges
on this page, it was designed
by TY Lin International.*

ROADWAY   STAY CABLES

STEP BY STEP

9 When the structure of
the bridge is complete,
lights and safety rails are
added. Finally, traffic can
drive safely across.

39

Bridge Facts

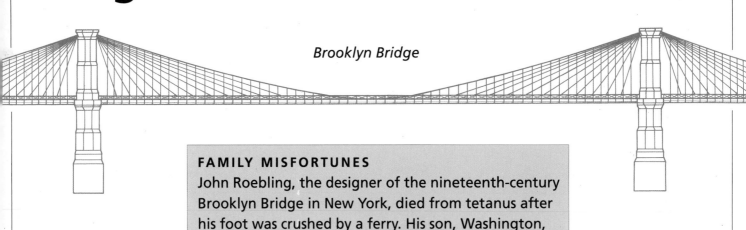

Brooklyn Bridge

FAMILY MISFORTUNES
John Roebling, the designer of the nineteenth-century Brooklyn Bridge in New York, died from tetanus after his foot was crushed by a ferry. His son, Washington, took over but was paralyzed by the bends after working on one of the bridge's caissons.

Chesapeake Bay Bridge-Tunnel

BRIDGE OR TUNNEL?
The Chesapeake Bay Bridge-Tunnel, linking two parts of Virginia, is 17 miles (28km) long. It includes 12 miles (19km) of viaduct, two high-level bridges to allow ships to pass, and two tunnels.

Sydney Harbour Bridge

WORLD'S WIDEST
The Sydney Harbour Bridge, Australia, has the widest deck of any bridge. There are six lanes of traffic, two railroad tracks, a bicycle track, and a sidewalk.

London Bridge One

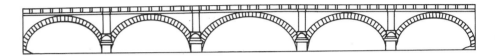

London Bridge Two

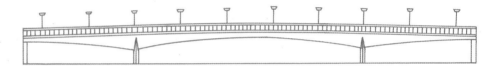

London Bridge Three

ONE...

The first London Bridge, across the Thames River, was built in 1209. It was covered with houses, shops, and inns.

TWO...

A second bridge replaced the first in 1831. It had five arches compared with the original's nineteen.

THREE

A third London Bridge with only three arches was built in the 1970s. The second bridge was taken apart and rebuilt in Arizona.

LOST LIVES

Eighty-seven lives were lost during the construction of the Quebec Bridge, Canada. In 1916, the central span fell into the river. The bridge took 18 years to complete.

Quebec Bridge

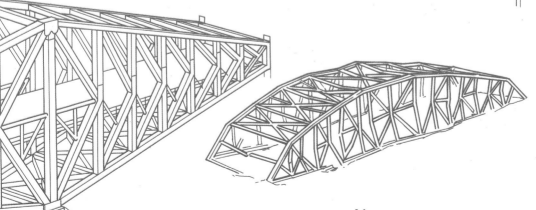

Time Chart

See how bridges have developed over the centuries with this time chart. The chart shows key bridges around the world and when they were built.

c stands for circa, which means about. It is used before dates that may not be accurate.

10,000 BC
People begin to live in settlements. This is probably when the world's first bridges were built.

FIRST CENTURY AD
The Romans build the Pont du Gard aqueduct near Nîmes, southern France.

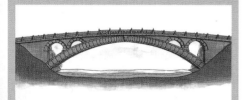

610
The Anji Bridge is built from stone in Zhoa Xian, China. It is one of the first long, low arch bridges in the world.

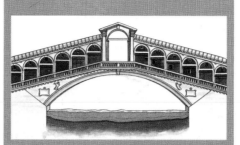

1591
The Rialto Bridge, Venice, is completed. It is one of the first long, low arch bridges of the European Renaissance.

1779
The first iron bridge in the world is built at Coalbrookdale in Shropshire, England.

1805
Thomas Telford builds the Pont-y-Cysyllte aqueduct, Wales. The canal water is held in a long iron trough.

1826
The Menai Straits Bridge, Wales, opens. It is a suspension bridge with cables made of iron chains. The span is 564 feet (172m) long.

1850
Robert Stephenson completes the Britannia Bridge, Wales, using iron tubes. It is the forerunner of the box girder bridge. The bridge's central span is 460 feet (140m) long.

1879
The cast-iron Tay Bridge, Scotland, collapses as a train crosses it in gale-force winds. Seventy-five people are killed.

1883
The Brooklyn Bridge, New York, is completed. It is the first suspension bridge to have steel cables. The bridge's central span is 1,590 feet (484m) long.

1890
The Forth Rail Bridge, Scotland, is completed. It is the world's first steel bridge. Each middle span is 1,700 feet (518m) long.

1894
Tower Bridge in London, England, is completed. It is a bascule bridge with two lifting cantilevers, which can be raised to let ships pass. The main span is 260 feet (79m) wide.

1917
The Quebec Bridge, Canada, is opened. It is a steel truss cantilever bridge, with a span of 1,800 feet (549m).

1932
The Sydney Harbour Bridge, Australia, is completed. It is a huge steel arch with a span of 1,650 feet (503m).

1937
The Golden Gate Bridge in San Francisco opens. Its central span is 4,200 feet (1,280m) long.

1940
The Tacoma Narrows Bridge, Washington, collapses in a strong wind. It was the world's third longest bridge.

1981
The world's longest suspension bridge, the Humber Bridge, England, is opened. Its overall length is 7,285 feet (2,220m).

1995
The Pont de Normandie, France, opens. It is the world's longest cable-stayed bridge, with a central span of 2,808 feet (856m).

1998
The Akashi Kaikyo Bridge, Japan, is due to open, linking the islands of Honshu and Shikoku. It will be the world's longest bridge, with a central span of 6,530 feet (1,990m).

2004
The Messina Strait Bridge between Sicily and Italy may open. It will have a total span of 10,830 feet (3,300m).

From Start to Finish

On these two pages, you can follow the Step by Step stories in the bottom right-hand corner of each double page from start to finish.

BUILDING A CONCRETE ROAD BRIDGE

1 Before bridge building can start, geologists must survey the site. They test the ground by drilling boreholes with a rig.

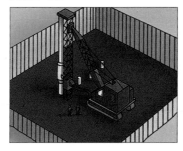

2 Watertight cofferdams are built in the riverbed. These keep the water out while engineers build the bridge's pile foundations.

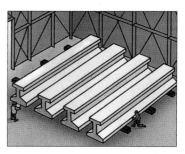

3 Massive prestressed concrete beams for the bridge are manufactured in a factory and later transported to the site.

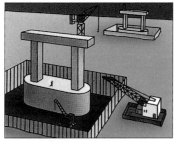

4 Concrete piers for the new bridge are built on top of the pile foundations that have been driven deep into the riverbed.

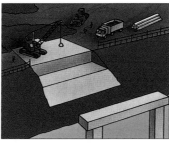

5 Massive concrete abutments are built on both the riverbanks to provide strong support for the bridge beams.

6 The concrete side beams are lifted into place by huge cranes working from the riverbanks. Slowly, the bridge is taking shape.

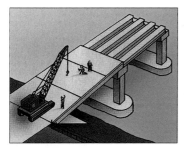

7 Once the side beams are securely in place, the deck can be added over them. It is constructed using in situ concrete.

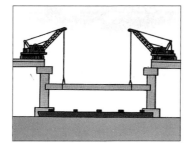

8 Once the deck covers the side beams, the central span beams are lifted up from a barge in the river by cranes.

9 The deck is completed, and safety rails, lights, signs, and lane markings are all added. Finally the bridge is opened to traffic.

BUILDING A CABLE-STAYED BRIDGE

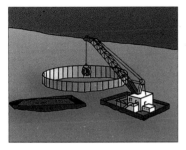

1 The foundations are built inside caissons that have been sunk to the riverbed. Supporting piers are built on top of the foundations.

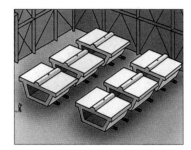

2 Concrete sections for the bridge's deck are built in a factory. Their aerodynamic shape stops the bridge from swaying.

3 The first sections of the bridge's deck are built on top of the piers. These will provide a base for the bridge towers.

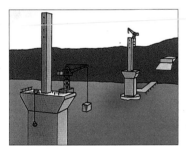

4 The towers are built section by section on top of the piers. They will carry the bridge's weight down to the ground.

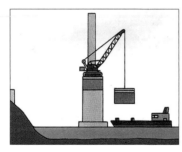

5 More sections of the deck are put into place on either side of the towers. Cranes lift them from barges in the river.

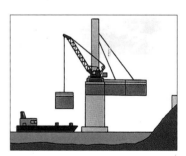

6 Each section of the deck is connected to one of the bridge cables, which in turn is connected to a tower.

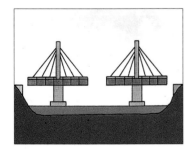

7 More sections of the deck are added piece by piece around each tower, until the roadway is almost complete.

8 The deck has to be covered with asphalt to prepare it for heavy traffic. This is done by a special paving machine.

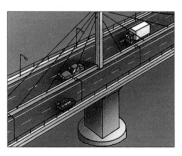

9 When the structure of the bridge is complete, lights and safety rails are added. Finally, traffic can drive safely across.

Glossary

abutment A support at the end of a bridge.

aerodynamic Describes a shape that uses the wind to its advantage, for example, to hold it in place.

aggregate Broken or crushed stone.

alloy A metal-like substance made by mixing a metal with other chemicals.

anchor A place where suspension bridge cables are firmly attached to the ground. The anchor can be natural rock or a huge concrete block.

approach road A road that leads to or from a bridge.

asphalt An oily, waterproof substance mixed with small stones to make a road surface.

ballast Heavy material, such as concrete, rock, or water, used to weigh down an object.

bedrock Solid rock buried under layers of softer rock or soil.

borehole A hole drilled into the ground to investigate the soil and rocks beneath the surface.

box girder A beam with a cross section in the shape of a box, made from concrete or by welding together steel plates.

cast iron Iron made into shapes by pouring molten iron into molds. Cast iron is hard but brittle.

centering A wooden arch constructed to support the blocks of an arch bridge until the arch is complete.

cofferdam A temporary, watertight, circular dam that allows foundation work to be carried out on a riverbed.

compression The squeezing together of a substance. An object that is pressed on both ends is in compression.

deck The roadway of a bridge.

detour A route between two places that is longer than the shortest possible route.

dredger A floating machine that removes silt from a riverbed. Some dredgers dig with buckets and some suck up silt like a giant vacuum cleaner.

duct A long, narrow hole along which wires or cables are threaded.

formwork A wood or metal mold into which concrete is poured to make a concrete structure.

foundations Parts of the supports of a bridge that spread the weight of the bridge into the ground. Foundations are normally under the ground.

geology *1.* The study of the rocks and how they are formed. *2.* The type of rock or soil at a place and how it is arranged.

hanger A cable or rod on which the deck of a suspension or arch bridge hangs.

high-tensile steel Steel that has been specially treated to make it much stronger in tension than normal steel.

in situ concrete Concrete that is molded on a building site rather than in a factory.

Industrial Revolution The period from about 1750 to about 1850 when industries started to grow in Europe, and roads and railroads began to be built.

key The final section to be added to a beam or arch bridge that is built in sections.

lattice girder A steel or iron beam that has a plate girder along its top and bottom edges, linked by a crisscross pattern of struts and ties.

masonry Stone, brick, or concrete.

millennium A thousand year period (the first millennium started in the year AD 1, the second in the year AD 1001), or the change from one millennium to the next.

pendulum A pole or string that has a weight at its bottom end and can swing freely.

pier A support that holds up a bridge's deck from underneath. Piers support the bridge away from the abutments at its ends.

pile A steel or concrete column reaching down to solid rock under layers of soft soil.

precast concrete Concrete that is formed into its final shape in a factory rather than on the building site where it will be used.

raft A type of foundation with a large slab of concrete, that "floats" on the ground. A raft or "floating" is used where piles would be impractical.

silt Sandy particles that are washed down a river. When the river gets wider and slower, the particles settle on its bed, making thick layers.

smelting Melting an ore, or a rock containing metal, to extract the metal from it. For example, iron is extracted from iron ore.

span The distance from one support of a bridge to the next. The span given for a bridge is normally for the longest unsupported section. For example, the distance between the towers of a suspension bridge is its span.

strut A part of a truss that gets pushed at both ends, so it is in compression, when the truss has a load on it.

tension The pulling apart of a substance. An object that is pulled at both ends is in tension.

tie A part of a truss that gets pulled at both ends, so it is in tension, when the truss has a load on it.

truss A strong framework of straight sections of metal (called struts and ties) joined together at their ends.

truss girder A truss that acts as a beam in a bridge.

viaduct A long bridge supported by many piers or arches that crosses a wide valley.

weld A way of joining two pieces of metal by adding molten metal between them, or by melting the edges of the pieces of metal so they fuse together.

winch A machine that pulls a rope or cable in order to lift or pull an object.

wrought iron Iron that is much more pure than cast iron and is better for use in structures because it is less brittle.

Index

Words in **bold** appear in the glossary on pages 46 and 47.